Where all the Birds Are Dancing

poems by

S. J. Stephens

Finishing Line Press
Georgetown, Kentucky

Where all the Birds Are Dancing

For my unfailingly supportive parents Jean Marie and Charles Stephens. Among your many gifts, you gave me a passion for life, unconditional love, and the courage to follow my dreams.

"It was the spirit of poetry who reached out and found me as I stood there at the doorway between panic and love."
—Joy Harjo, Crazy Brave: A Memoir

Copyright © 2020 by S. J. Stephens
ISBN 978-1-64662-299-3 First Edition
All rights reserved under International and Pan-American Copyright Conventions. No part of this book may be reproduced in any manner whatsoever without written permission from the publisher, except in the case of brief quotations embodied in critical articles and reviews.

ACKNOWLEDGMENTS

"Forgotten Things" in *Licking River Review* Literary Magazine, "Diminishing Brilliance;" "The River Runs Too Deep;" "Complicit Not Consensual" in *For a Better World*, Greater Cincinnati Artists.
"If I Could Fly," originally published as "Hidden Among Trees" in *Sugared Water* Literary Magazine.

Publisher: Leah Maines
Editor: Christen Kincaid
Cover Art: Shari Rust
Author Photo: S. J. Stephens
Cover Design: Elizabeth Maines McCleavy

Order online: www.finishinglinepress.com
also available on amazon.com

Author inquiries and mail orders:
Finishing Line Press
P. O. Box 1626
Georgetown, Kentucky 40324
U. S. A.

Table of Contents

All the Dancing Birds	1
The River Runs Too Deep	2
Hunger in the Churning	3
The Cusp	4
Clipped Away	5
In the Churning	6
Diminishing Brilliance	7
Ohio Morning	9
An Image of Peace	10
Bones Long to Sing	12
Squirreling Them Away	13
In the Pulse	14
I am the Battlefield	15
This City is She	16
Handfuls of Light	17
Shadow Birth	18
If I Could Fly	19
Waiting for Children	20
Mother	21
Strange Ideas	22
Perpetuating	23
Complicit Not Consensual	24
First World Woman	25
Finding Balance	26
Small Town October Nights	27
It Takes Succulence	28
Backyard Monument	29
Desire Only Leaves Things Behind	30
Forgotten Things	31
From My Window	32
Unexpected Beauty	33
Insomnia	34
Pieces That Matter	35
What Remains	36

All the Dancing Birds

The red plucked belly of a bird at slaughter
eats without joy
without pleasure.

Confusion her only companion as friends
run headless around the yard
bumping into stone children and wood nymphs.

My grandmother watches
sitting in the window
her legs are crossed.

All good girls cross their legs to hide the secret
the open dripping heart
that runs red with sorrow.

She can't save her children from the massacre that lies in the yard.
They've finished dancing and wait in the grass
for men to turn death to food.

Feed the children
it is her duty after all, to feed the children
to feed husband, and neighbor.

To feed the traditions who impose expectations on her blood.
The red follows her, trails behind
as she prepares the meal that eats her from the inside.

Following the feed
she becomes plucked and raw, red and rewarded.
Still, she watches from the window

where all the birds are dancing.

The River Runs Too Deep

I wear the impression of Cinderella and her feminist rant
like an evening gown.
My glass slippers pinch to pay the price of beauty
or the price of fitting into the river ideology
and when we've had enough
we're chased and shaped.
The essence diluted and dumped into the rigid
like leaves that float with the current.
Pulled spine and bones from the river
the framework identity, intact
like blue that flows silk to the floor.

Hunger in the Churning

Like birds in the morning who wake to the hunger of hymn,
sing a song of legacy.

The call of God lolls in potential flaws,
with blood in veins; to heart, and lung, and brain.

The essential beating doesn't know it's alive
but hears my own ferocious yearning

in the unsung,
in lyrics that hide in infinitesimal spaces.

A chorus agitates the silence—
cloaked in the calm of a mind at rest.

Feign the energy, an echo
deny the fever, the holy lust.

A furious appetite consumes,
the song nurtured, and… Inflamed.

The Cusp

I sit at the precipice
as dew on the tip of a wing
or a branch bent by strong wind.
I remember a time when excitement filled me at new beginnings.
When my heart raced to the speed of dancing
and music played in my veins.
I remember a time before this plague blew in from my bowels, burnt,
burning ashes that rest without sleep.
I remember a time before chest pain hammered
through the words of the Goddess. Her beauty
blind inspiration and I feel the wind whip the tiny hairs on my body
to meet her challenge.
I remember a time before she whispered too low to hear
and I fear taking a step into the undefined space
a void with no name or light or sound.
I remember a time before
the space between me and the waiting.
I remember a time before the cusp.

Clipped Away

The rock formation in *The Cliff, Étretat, Sunset*
chases the red sun as it descends,
it never loses light or shadow.
The coast of Oregon in summer

asks me to have faith in the unyielding,
I don't know if I believe in prayer,
though it works for my mother.
When I delve into the painting

I can hear the ocean, feel the cool breeze
where rocks rise and stand still amid the waves.
Natural forces take pieces out to sea
in the changing tides of summer.

I read that Scientists searched for the exact
date and time Monet painted,
the precise spot where he stood.
As if mortals could really know a God,

as if static moments remain still,
as if the changing tide and wind hadn't moved that rock,
as if the color of the sun didn't change
and the sea hadn't clipped away at Normandy.

In the Churning

These words,
    hollow words
        that die in the damp dark
            shame and desire become a fiction
                to we who incandesce

Churning like blood
    crucial and contaminated
        let's learn from that desire
            let's cry in the dark vibrating matter
                below the distraction of things

An echo of pain perceived
    shudder in waves
        reach into the shadow
            no release, no reprieve
                a constant pulsing

I do not fully grasp the violence
    burned energy becomes
        a haunting—visible and the invisible
            before understanding the alchemy
                casting off the husk of imbedded creed

My flesh is not callow
    it's false to crave the convergence
        a rawness climbs out
            wet with new understanding
                howls, enraged beyond fear and shame

It has been my instinct to suppress
    thunder—cringe in shame
        drown in my own liquid
            as if trapped
                until the hunger sings

Draw up a chord to heaven
    shame so shrill it makes me shudder
        a raw and bloody fear rises in me
            it runs deep
                but there is also, wild wild joy

Diminishing Brilliance

Hyacinth Macaw poached and caged
in the Salty Dog Café. Born a wild thing, captured
Her predator's claws rip her underbelly clean
leaving a blue scattered ground of glory
where children steal in to find treasure lost in slurry
She watches with the madness of captivity

What humanity has bred this careless custody
Who pride themselves on their civilized cage
Patrons ignore the filth
of magnificence captured
And in precious vestige of her pallid brilliance
somehow their blood runs clean

of narrow minds unwashed
in their own captivity
As they swim in the currency of her luminosity
I claim this exotic bird caged
and rage against its capture
Bathed in the grime

of unconcerned immoral waste
of a creature scrubbed
and netted
In her depraved captivity
the depth of my compassion is caged
and I ache with her in solidarity of lost glory

The diminishing of her brilliance
in blue feathers floating into the refuse
vicious disdain sells t-shirts to cage
the brilliant, lost, and unclean.
A new kind of feral in her captivity
our depravity captured

in innocent souvenirs children captured
a foreshadow of their harvest homage
that will be held in captivity
as they wade through the filth
and beg to be clean
and free instead of a gilded caged

Finally, aware of humanity caged
in the choice of unclean
choices, we are lost in the filth

Ohio Morning

The Ohio River winds along the road I travel,
flooding trees on the bank.
Their barren branches reach out to me
as if begging for life.
The bark itches where it buds,
like the pain
of a childless mother.
Dreaming to be Daphne
—the Laurel with a beating heart.
At least she was filled,
filled by God.

An Image of Peace

In the company of many, succulence is hidden.
What wings can hide the splendor of essence
inside this flock of burden? Rise high in waiting,
the closer the bird, the more shrouded the image of peace
until the messenger drops his head in surrender,
and carries the dead home to the living.

This temporary home is not a place for living,
and in the masses our deaths are hidden.
What choice do we have but to surrender
the feathers that fall when we rise, our essence?
They fall in anticipation of peace,
so we despair of what is lost in waiting.

There is no calm or beauty in this waiting,
and our hearts beat wild to be living.
The anticipation of life restores the peace,
but still, promise remains hidden.
Our message lost in rising essence,
but the spirit within refuses to surrender.

Among the offering of scattered seed, you expect surrender,
we hope you don't mind the waiting.
We'll take your sustenance but won't leave our essence.
Instead it is passed from the dead to the living.
Is our message so far hidden?
It should be easy to find a small semblance of peace,

in our commonness there is beauty and peace.
Our wings spread and to the sky we surrender,
as in volume, singular colors are hidden.
Looking down, the others are still waiting,
for seeds to be spread to the living.
And in this waiting, we forage for new essence,

for the sweetness of purpose is in essence.
Our exhausting quest for a truth in finding peace,
the proof of this presence is living.
To understand we must surrender
to the horrors ahead, they are waiting.
We see them in plain sight, where they are hidden,

and it is the sweetest surrender,
to fly high where our god is waiting,
to fly beyond where the colors of truth are hidden.

Bones Long to Sing

Trying to reach bones that long to sing
I get caught on the webbed feet of the duck
who walks toward the lake
and wish the wind wouldn't whip
every molecule against my skin
My feet are bare
they blister
and I burn to ash

Squirreling Them Away

It wasn't the gun that killed them,
it was our world that picked at their souls
like scavenger birds feasting.

I think about my students who can't be bored for a moment
before the flash of light is reflected in their glasses,
I can't fascinate all the time.

They squirrel away precious life while we
struggle to make sense of the trophies and ribbons,
of straight A report cards and a volunteer pin.

All relics of the teens still bleeding in the schools.
I was that teen though less accomplished,
with the feeling of being alone in a world full of people.

It's not about being loved or failures and accomplishments
or status on the team,
it is the hole left by the ephemeral

programed into their brains.
We forget to fill them with God and beauty, instead
we put the gun and the pills under their pillows.

In the Pulse

in the pulse
my first glimpse
a swift kick of afternoon haze
in the heat of hummingbirds hovering
search for the nectar it takes to survive
trust the clouds
when a vanishing space has spent its influence
my body echoes purpose
in the slow hour
there is more than this to gain

I am the Battlefield

We don't need heroes to remember love
they only seduce us with smiles and strength
forget us
before the next sacrifice.

I am the battlefield.
Tongue left wet
to put out this fire,

Where air is cold between us,
feed on tenderness
until we become the feast,

and find the light.
We won't fall into the spectacle
it releases parachutes
before we fall

like the wing of a blue macaw
taking flight.

This City Is She

Earth moves this city
three inches to the left

She might sink into the ocean
feeding diatoms
releasing oxygen into the atmosphere

She doesn't harness the sun

She could be cirrostratus
could show me God
or the antithesis of God

In a milky blue veil
she doesn't shift the sky
but a halo forms around her

Mother bird regurg—feeding her craze
protecting her from pills and booze
keeping her safe

Handfuls of Light

Blue sky meets the blue ocean in the distance
it roars against the sand

the wind whisks salt into my hair
steals my rapture—replaces it with sorrow

my lips and skin sticky as if drenched in sugar.
I catch handfuls of light—mistake it for a blessing

while warmth escapes through my fingertips.
I wait for turtles to descend from the sea

to watch them plant babies in the marsh
to carry tradition to the next generation.

Waiting for the spirit of blessings to find me
I need to be filled by the sacred.

Those turtles will come
I will witness some kind of birth.

Shadow Birth

I flatter dirt
and trust the crack of chance in clouds.
I pursue the slow hour
my body echoes.
I woo the wind
my first glimpse—a swift kick of afternoon haze.
I court iron embryos
left when a vanishing space has spent its influence.
The milieus of gulley encounters
a black mark on a white dove's branch,
the soft wing of sight.
My palms deep
in the pulse of hummingbirds hovering,
left, an empty nest
to be birthed.

If I Could Fly

Methuselah hides from me among her peers,
where ancient trees tower,
spread their seed
with bristlecone pine.
A target drawn on my chest waits patiently
for an embryo to sow
any small kernel might sink into my belly,
soothe my spirit, waiting
for branches to grow wings.

If I could fly as high as a Redwood
I would cultivate a brood in lichen
and restore my bountiful truth.
At the core, my mother's milk
runs dry despite tenderness.
Heavy fog on steep branches,
clings to cones that fight as they fall
wasted.

Waiting for Children

Wind blew across the top of the water
To observe the goose atop its nest,

There she waits for children to emerge.
Waiting to renew faith in instinct
and the purpose of life.

She watched for predators,
the men who cracked her eggs once.
Sent her children to a watery grave.

Those unlived babies still swell
in her breast. She wonders,
where are my babies.

Mother

I can't tell the difference between us
in the images I place on the wall

In a world not made for either of us, we make
shadows to cast against our blue wall

You love that blue wall and drink
wine in a glass full of deep red

We cast a line out past the geese
beyond what we can see
and the black crow perches on a Sugar Maple

I sweep the ground to collect feathers
while children splash their feet
in the cool murk of the bank

Strange Ideas

In the summer, in the country at night
The air thick with crickets' song
Pure in the space of my memories
The magic

He rolled on top of me
Took my breath in his mouth
Touched the limits of experience
Took things I had no name for

Teenage boys have strange ideas about love
—they kiss you in parking lots
on park benches
And on the driveway at 3am

Perpetuating

I rage at radio announcers who think Louis C.K.
should be allowed to earn his living
doing "what he loves and is good at"

> We aren't peahens, we don't want
> a show, keep your flamboyant feathers
> in your pants

"Should he have to pay
the rest of his life for one mistake?"
Fuck Yes. He should pay

> Rape culture bastards who accept his display
> Of extravagance in the shelter of his authority
> spin their iridescence, in the face of our innocence

I don't know if you know, you raped me
But I know you violated me
And changed my humanity

Complicit Not Consensual

I.
I don't know if you're a rapist,
But I know that I said no
Five times, the memory is vivid.

You took my virginity in a drunken brawl
Tearing me in half
I left your half in a pool of blood on your bed

When I returned to collect it
You'd thrown it out with other unwanted things
So I left the contents of my stomach

II.
Sixteen years
the smell of your apartment,

your breath,
the brutal weight of you,

the feeling of you inside me
blood that ran copper down the drain,

fresh like flowers after rain.
Memories are ripped from me when others speak their rape.

III.
Sometimes, I'm angry

at the confusion rattled by memories when I think of you
at the guilt I feel in my complicity
at allowing you to touch me

at how I enjoyed your kisses and your hands on my body
at the innocence I willingly placed in your hands
at my need to not be raped.

First World Woman

Who deserve
flooded apartments
cats with broken legs
faithless men
fickle friends
Desire bores a hole
carpenter bees nest in the center

Finding Balance

When power collides with grace—
you must choose to win and be great
or to fly or walk
among those who have chosen

Elegance strikes a balance with capability
sparks a new debate between real and could be—
dreams that work and aren't real
but define real as actual or authentic

We meet at potential and poised—
to see again the collision that smashes
grace and feeds power, and pretends
courteous influence we don't understand

See how we change when we choose—
the capable over the honor. We crave
to understand the struggle, but it
keeps at us with electric claws

Before we can determine respect—
it collapses decency or righteousness.
In strength it fights for more than a choice
more than power—more than grace

Small Town October Nights

Small town Ohio full of fireflies in late October
The night filled with their light
You can watch them over the lake
No bigger than a creek
Where my father fished as a child

The fish are fat in the lake
Only the fingerlings jump to catch lightning
This Indian summer mist rises
As daytime heat cools to an autumn night
Sparks in the fog like vision after a head injury

It feels like ecstasy
Spiritual, as if God has shed light
In those small flecks of fire that glow
Children chase them across the lawn
Collect them like stars in jars on the nightstand

If I could draw or paint, it would be this late fall
Before wind blows and takes the light
Color and shape
Glowing of insects across the lake

I release the fire back into the sky
And empty the dead on the grass

It Takes Succulence

He asked, *Are you Romantic*
She said, *I'm not Snow White*

        If you let me I will steal your pith
        stash it in my pocket
        while the earth withers

        It takes succulence
        Like raindrops on my cheek
        But that doesn't fit in a pocket

Backyard Monument

The rosebuds you gave me,
dead
bend like a crimson congregation bowed in prayer.

I touch the shriveled edges to my,
lips
breathe the scattered petals.

A mocking bird sings a scoffing
song.
I wear a black veil to the ceremony

where I kneel before the monument
bury
the dead in the yard to cultivate.

Desire Leaves Things Behind

Desire only leaves things behind
It left a necklace made of blue glass

Burned edges of flower petals
And a ticket stub

When the clock stops its empty minutes
I think about the children who run to be running

Set the sun on the dresser,
Put away diamond earrings

And that locket I found at a rummage sale.
It's stuck in an old wooden jewelry box—

Cedar drifts from the inside
Smells of fire and exotic dreams,
Everything else, ordinary.

Forgotten Things

I crack open my chest
gift wrap the contents
and lay it at your feet

You take it casually
fling it aside
like other forgotten things

It seeps from the edges
like a bruise
heat gathers beneath my skin.

As if it weren't a kind of madness,
it blinds
like looking directly into the sun

From my Window

Honeysuckle climbs the fence behind my house,
divides cultivated grass from wild.

The Honeysuckle bloomed last week,
it's December and the rain tricked the twine with warmth.

Today, Honeysuckle ovoids freeze and crystalize nectar,
With no oil to anoint the body, no marrow to suck.

Leaves fall in sacred water
that winds around the yellow excavator.

It interrupts the blue of the horizon,
sounding off its metallic cry and I am

lost in waste from the careless offshoots,
who push against my serenity.

Unexpected Beauty

Low hung fog gathers over the Ohio
It's mid-morning in January and the temperature changed
from seven degrees yesterday to fifty-three degrees today

The rain soaks gray chunks of snow collected along the highway
they are companions to a mess of twisted metal and dead animals
It's the same road I've driven a thousand times in forty years
and still I don't always recognize my way home

The fog dissipates into the atmosphere
pieces amass in the clouds and fall to the ground
It will fall and tomorrow among the metal and
the carcass of a coyote I've been watching for several days

It doesn't belong among the natural landscape
interrupted by the concrete and asphalt
Somehow it becomes apart of the beauty
as death births new life in the spring

Insomnia

Did I survive the Fall?
I ask the no one sleeping in my bed.
We laugh and the cat scratches my face.

We don't sleep at night,
or any night the lights shine through the window,
artificial like the neon store lights that disfigure me.

I breathe in before opening the window,
the air is too cold.
I add a blanket to my bed.

Still we don't sleep.
It isn't the minutes I fear,
it's fickle nature of the morning.

Pieces That Matter

The way lips curve in a slow smile reminds me of my first love. He was beautiful and cruel and stunning and kind. He was the wave that retreats from the shore as quickly as it arrives but above all else he wasn't mine to love. Memories are like that, as rare as Pyura (blood rock). They have a heart that beats or at least a motion within, a kind of clear blood, a hermaphroditic delicacy that resembles toxin, a silvery-gray elemental metal that can be shaped on the inside. Those memories are malleable and I wonder about the Trans kid who lives down the street. He went to his first pride parade to find love. He found acceptance in mothers and fathers with hugs to spare. In a space of more than tolerance, he found sustenance. We feed this affection so we can reduce the infection of hatred, the kind he found at home. His parents allow him to live in the basement, and call him Edith to their friends. Pretend like Eddie doesn't exist. Their tenderness lost where he forms the living rock, it bleeds not quite as pure as the young boy's tears. So, I think about my grand love that imitated passion like Pyura imitates rock, and know appearance is a small fraction of the whole, where the heart cannot be distilled into pieces of matter.

What Remains

I haven't forgotten the wooden dollhouse
you built for us in shop class
it scratches my memory like time
I haven't forgotten that Fourth of July
when my hair went up like a fire cracker
Dad always made us keep it long
and the singed edges shaped me
outside of his expectations but the
scent was sweet and I wasn't afraid

I haven't forgotten the way your hands fit
into father's gloves, the ones left after
Christmas brought him a new pair
You loved the worn leather and didn't care
if it was pig skin or goat
Dad always wore goat
Even though the love lies on the floor
with sawdust and drops of paint
and years of words stick in the cracks of wood paneling

I remember the dollhouse and that's almost enough

www.ingramcontent.com/pod-product-compliance
Lightning Source LLC
LaVergne TN
LVHW041559070426
835507LV00011B/1179